woman

All Things New

DEVOTIONAL BOOK

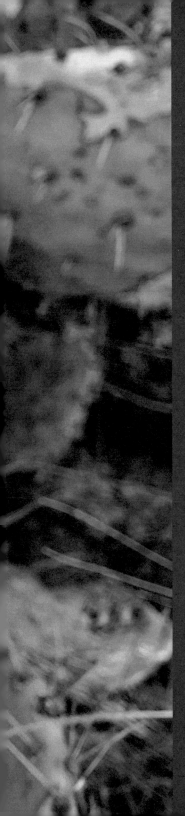

DEVO:
KATY BEZET & BECKY BARBER
DAUGHTER   MOM

There was a moment a few years ago when I found myself drowning. Not literally; but figuratively, I was drowning on the inside. I felt overwhelmed, overpowered, and like the waters were closing in and I was desperate for the Lord's help. I remember being face-to-the-carpet, crying out for God to help me, and somehow I ended up in Psalm 18, where David seems to be in a similar state of desperation. It was there that I found a lifeline of hope to grasp onto:

> *"He reached down from on high and took hold of me;*
> *he drew me out of deep waters.*
> *He rescued me from my powerful enemy,*
> *from my foes, who were too strong for me."*
>
> **Psalm 18:16-17**

The imagery of God reaching into my chaos to rescue me when I was about to sink speaks directly to my heart still today. And in the passage we're focusing on this week, Isaiah 43:1-7, we see this same characteristic of God on display: He is our Redeemer.

Isaiah 43:1 says, *"Do not fear, for I have redeemed you."*

Redeem is a word we don't use much, aside from redeeming a coupon at Kroger. But in the Biblical context, the word "redeem" is rich and full of meaning that helps us understand who the Lord is. Redeem means to buy back, to release from captivity—to rescue. He is the one who has rescued us from sin and darkness and offered us life and freedom through Jesus.

> *"When you pass through the waters,*
> *I will be with you;*
> *and when you pass through the rivers,*
> *they will not sweep over you.*
> *When you walk through the fire,*
> *you will not be burned;*
> *the flames will not set you ablaze."*
> **Isaiah 43:2**

Reading this verse calls to memory the Old Testament stories of the Israelites enduring some impossible opposition, only to prevail against all odds. With the help of God's mighty hand, the Israelites passed through the waters of the Red Sea while the enemy was swallowed up in the waves (Exodus 14). Another time, three Israelite young men, Shadrach, Meschach, and Abednego, were put to the test in the fiery furnace, but they came out unscathed and not even smelling like fire (Daniel 3). Truly, the Lord was with them in the raging waters and the blazing fire.

But do these verses about passing through the waters and fire apply to you? Absolutely—they apply to your life because you are one of God's own. And He is faithful to you,

His daughter, just as He was faithful in the stories of old! He is the same Redeemer to the people of Israel as He is to us 2,000 years later. We may not need to be rescued from an actual fiery furnace, but many of us have walked through the fires of rejection or misunderstanding. We have fought against the raging waters of fear and depression that seek to swallow us up. We have been on the brink of drowning in one way or another.

If you find yourself in a desperate situation where you need the Lord to reach out and save you, take heart:

Psalm 107:19-21 *"Then they cried to the Lord in their trouble, and he saved them from their distress. He sent out his word and healed them; he rescued them from the grave. Let them give thanks to the Lord for his unfailing love and his wonderful deeds for mankind."*

Colossians 1:13-14 *"For he has rescued us from the dominion of darkness and brought us into the kingdom of the Son he loves, in whom we have redemption, the forgiveness of sins."*

Following Jesus does not exempt us from walking through hardship in life. But following Jesus will change the way we walk. As believers, we can walk through difficulty with hope because God is in control. We can walk through trials with peace because we literally have the Prince of Peace living within us (Isaiah 9:6).

When you read this section of Isaiah 43:1-7, the way God speaks to His people is beautiful. He says, "I have called you by your name; you are mine," and "you are precious in my sight, and honored, and I love you." God speaks the same words to you today: He knows you by name, He created you, He formed you, and you are His! The Lord's eyes are fixed on you, and you are precious to Him. He loves you!

 REFLECTION:

1. Share a time when the Lord rescued you from something (whether physical, emotional, spiritual, etc.).
2. Think about the people you see on a day-to-day basis (friends, co-workers, family). How can you share God's faithfulness in your life with others? How might your story of "rescue" impact their lives?
3. Is there an area in your life where you need God to redeem you? Revisit the definition of "redeem" and think about how you are believing in the Lord to continue moving in your life.
4. God says He created you, knows you deeply, and you are precious in His sight. Do you fully believe this? Stop and pray, "Lord, I give You my heart. Help me to trust You with everything in my life—big and small."

PRAYER:

Thank You, Lord, that You created me, formed me, and love me. Help me to fully grasp how much You care for me. God, I surrender my life to You. I give You every instance where circumstances seem overwhelming. I invite You to be Lord of every area of my life. God, would You help me have a heart that yields to You in every circumstance. I trust You, Lord, with my future!

REMEMBER NOT THE FORMER THINGS, NOR CONSIDER THE THINGS OF OLD. BEHOLD, I AM DOING A NEW THING; NOW IT SPRINGS FORTH, DO YOU NOT PERCEIVE IT? I WILL MAKE A WAY IN THE WILDERNESS AND RIVERS IN THE DESERT.
ISAIAH 43:18-19

REMEMBER NOT THE FORMER THINGS, NOR CONSIDER THE THINGS OF OLD. BEHOLD, I AM DOING A NEW THING;
NOW IT SPRINGS FORTH, DO YOU NOT PERCEIVE IT? I WILL MAKE A WAY IN THE WILDERNESS AND RIVERS IN THE DESERT.
ISAIAH 43:18-19

ISAIAH 43:8-13

DEVO:
NICHEYTA RAINO & DONNA RAINO
DAUGHTER   MOM

Have you ever experienced a time when life felt completely out of sorts? Like when your local grocery store randomly decides to rearrange everything, and now it takes you 15 minutes to find the bread aisle? Or when you're running late for an appointment, you forget you left water boiling on the stove, the fire alarm is beeping, and you find your keys in the refrigerator? (True story.) We've all had those crazy moments.

But what about those other moments? Unexpected illness, family conflict, work stress, political unrest, financial uncertainty, raising children, crises of faith—the kinds of seasons that feel like a storm of chaos where questions outnumber answers, pain and doubt overshadow joy, and tears become constant companions? I remember experiencing a time like this a few years back. Maybe for you, it was last year or a few months ago. Perhaps you're in the middle of it right now. Friend, let me encourage you: no matter how impossible or uncertain your circumstances seem, God is still on His throne. He is for you, and He is with you.

As we read further into Isaiah 43, it's crucial to understand the context. The Israelites were enduring their own storm of chaos. They had experienced war, were captured by the Babylonians, and were exiled from their home. It was a period of intense heartache, suffering, and uncertainty. In this desperate situation, God spoke through Isaiah, reminding them of His unmatched authority and sovereign power.

Isaiah 43:10-11 declares, *"'You are my witnesses,' says the Lord, 'and my servant whom I have chosen, so that you may know and believe me and understand that I am he. Before me no god was formed, nor will there be one after me. I, even I, am the Lord, and apart from me, there is no savior. I have revealed and saved and proclaimed—I, and not some foreign god among you. You are my witnesses,' declares the Lord, 'that I am God.'"*

This powerful declaration is a continuation of the promises spoken in verses 1-7, where God says, *"Do not fear, for I have redeemed you,"* and, *"Do not be afraid, for I am with you."* God wanted to remind them that even in their tumultuous circumstance, He was near, He was in control, and He alone would save them.

Here's the thing—they didn't see an immediate reprieve when Isaiah spoke these words. There was no split-the-sea moment or manna-from-heaven miracle. They were still captured, still in exile. What they had was the assurance of God's sovereignty and salvation.

I remember a time when I prayed for a split-the-sea moment, and it didn't come. Life was full of anxiety and uncertainty at every turn: an unexpected diagnosis, heartbreak, fear. I was desperately trying to put on a brave face and fix everything, but everything was slipping like sand through my fingers. The stress of trying to make it right and figure it out on my own was too much.

I remember I re-read a scripture I am very familiar with. John 16:33 says, *"I have told you these things, so that in me you may have peace. In this world you will have trouble. But take heart! I have overcome the world."*

Jesus told us it was going to get hard. And the promise isn't that He'll take the hard things away. The promise is for us to have peace in Him. It is for us to trust in His sovereignty and know that He has overcome, and is victorious over, the world.

God's sovereignty means that He is in complete control of everything. He has the ultimate power and authority, ensuring that His plans and purposes always prevail. The enemy will use things like fear, doubt, and unbelief to war against our faith and make us question God's authority. We may have intrusive thoughts like, "If God is good, why did this happen?" When everything around us is being shaken, it is imperative that we be anchored in the assurance of God's sovereignty. The One who created all things, knows all things, and rules over all things. Friends, we live in a fallen and broken world, and hard times will come. But we are the daughters of the true and living God. We will not be shaken if we stand on the truth of His word.

Psalm 103:19 *"The Lord has established his throne in heaven, and his kingdom rules over all."*

Romans 8:28 *"And we know that in all things God works for the good of those who love him, who have been called according to his purpose."*

Isaiah 43:10-12 *"'...Before me no god was formed, nor will there be one after me. I, even I, am the Lord, and apart from me there is no savior. I have revealed and saved and proclaimed—I, and not some foreign god among you. You are my witnesses,' declares the Lord, 'that I am God.'"*

IF YOU'RE ANYTHING LIKE ME, YOU'LL READ THIS AND THINK, THIS IS GOOD TO KNOW, BUT HOW DO I APPLY IT TO MY EVERYDAY LIFE? HERE ARE A FEW WAYS:

PRAYER: Start your day with a prayer, acknowledging God's sovereignty over your life. Ask for His guidance, wisdom, and peace throughout the day. You can pray the prayers that are in this study. I like praying scripture, especially the Psalms.

STUDY SCRIPTURE: Choose a few key scriptures about God's sovereignty and faithfulness. Read them out loud, write them on note cards, or set them as reminders on your phone.

BIBLICAL LIFE-GIVING COMMUNITY: Surround yourself with people who will walk with you and encourage you in all of life's seasons. Be in a community of people who are full of faith and will remind you that God is in control and you can trust Him.

Knowing God's word and understanding His sovereignty changes the way we navigate life's "storms of chaos." In every season, whether calm or chaotic, let us anchor our souls in the unwavering assurance that our God reigns. He has declared, saved, and proclaimed— He is our God, and apart from Him, there is no savior.

✳ REFLECTION:

1. Share a recent time when your life felt chaotic or out of your control. How did you respond? How did it affect your faith?
2. How did you see God working in the midst of the chaos, even if His actions weren't immediately clear to you? What did you learn about His sovereignty through that experience?
3. How do you deal with intrusive thoughts and doubts, such as, "If God is good, why did this happen?"
4. How does understanding God's sovereignty help you combat attacks from the enemy, such as fear, doubt, and unbelief?

✳ PRAYER:

Father, I honor the righteousness of Him who knew no sin and whose blood washes away all my sin. I have faced hardships and insurmountable obstacles, holding on to hope to sustain my faith. Thank You for helping me stand firm as Your daughter, even in difficult times, and for making me Your witness. Because You are faithful and have kept Your promises, I can trust You and share Your love with those in this world who do not yet know You. Let me remain resolute, unswayed by circumstances, trusting that You are in control and always with me.

Thank You for working all things together for the good of those who love You and are called according to Your purpose. Even when trials in life make me feel trapped, defeated, and outnumbered, this promise remains true. You reveal Your divine nature to those who may not know You by refining me through these trials of my faith, and I emerge from them as a purified witness for You. I pray I will always remember Your sovereignty and faithfulness, knowing I am your child, called out of darkness into Your marvelous light.

REMEMBER NOT THE FORMER THINGS, NOR CONSIDER THE THINGS OF OLD. BEHOLD, I AM DOING A NEW THING; NOW IT SPRINGS FORTH, DO YOU NOT PERCEIVE IT? I WILL MAKE A WAY IN THE WILDERNESS AND RIVERS IN THE DESERT.
ISAIAH 43:18-19

REMEMBER NOT THE FORMER THINGS, NOR CONSIDER THE THINGS OF OLD. BEHOLD, I AM DOING A NEW THING;
NOW IT SPRINGS FORTH, DO YOU NOT PERCEIVE IT? I WILL MAKE A WAY IN THE WILDERNESS AND RIVERS IN THE DESERT.
ISAIAH 43:18-19

ISAIAH 43:14-21

DEVO:
HAILEE FRUCHEY & MICHELLE BEZET
DAUGHTER   MOM

My mom and I were having a conversation over coffee about praying BIG prayers. She was telling me about how her mom, my Grammie, prayed fervently for all of her children to be followers of Jesus. Long story short, my Grammie left this earth too early and crossed over into eternity without seeing the faithfulness of her prayers. Now, 13 years later, my mom and I are getting to see her brothers walk out a relationship with the Lord—a prayer that we saw my Grammie believe for, now coming to fruition. God promises us that He will do a new thing. Bring forth water to dry lands. And that's where we pick up in Isaiah.

In this powerful passage from Isaiah, God speaks to His people with both a reminder of past deliverance and a promise of future restoration.

The context of these verses is the Babylonian exile, a period of great suffering and displacement for the Israelites. But here, God, through Isaiah, delivers a message of hope and transformation.

Verses 14-15: God as Redeemer and Creator

The passage begins with a declaration of God's identity: the Redeemer, the Holy One of Israel, the Creator, and the King. These titles remind us of God's sovereignty and His intimate involvement in the history and destiny of His people. He's not distant or detached, but actively working for their deliverance.

The titles of God always bring peace to my soul. Being in a crazy world, God's identity NEVER changes. What He promises us about His character is the same yesterday, today, and forever.

Verses 16-17: Remembering God's Past Deeds

God recalls the miraculous events of the Exodus, where He made a way through the sea and defeated the pursuing Egyptian army. This reminder is crucial. It's a testament to God's power and faithfulness. If God could deliver His people in such a dramatic way before, He can certainly do it again.

The longer we walk with the Lord, His faithfulness is shown to us time and time again. Things that used to rock our world can now serve as reminders of His past deeds, building our faith and bringing peace by eliminating worry, doubt, and stress.

Verses 18-19: A Call to Embrace the New

"Forget the former things; do not dwell on the past. See, I am doing a new thing!"

This is a call to shift our focus. While remembering God's past deeds is important, being anchored in the past can hinder us from perceiving and embracing the new works God is doing. God is a God of renewal and creativity, constantly bringing forth new life and new possibilities. The new thing God is doing may not always resemble past events, but it carries might proclaim His praise. Our lives, transformed by God's intervention and provision, are meant to reflect His glory.

So, in our lives, we might be praying prayers that seem like wastelands—dry, barren, and devoid of hope. But, Isaiah 43:14-21 encourages us to trust in God's ability to make a way where there seems to be no way.

- **Reflect on God's faithfulness:** When we are feeling dry in our prayer lives or walks with the Lord, we can recall the times when God has brought forth new water in what felt like wastelands. Let these memories propel your faith in His continued presence and power.

- **Look forward with hope:** We have to be in a posture to receive the new things God is doing in our lives. Being so fixated on the past can cause us to miss the new paths and streams He is creating for us now.

- **Proclaim His praise:** As we experience God's provision and guidance, let our response be one of praise. Sharing testimonies of God's faithfulness will encourage others!

✺ REFLECTION:

1. Reflect on times you have seen God's faithfulness in your life.
2. Is there a time in which someone you know prayed for something that they didn't get to see come to pass, but you did?
3. How can you look at things differently in order to prepare for the newness that is coming in your life?
4. Which one of these verses from Isaish can you declare to help your heart trust for something new?

✺ PRAYER:

Lord, thank You for Your word! You're my Redeemer, Holy One, Creator, and King! Thank You for Your faithfulness and for making all things new. Thank You for being with me in my wastelands, even when I don't see it or feel it. Help me to see things differently; to see things as You see them. I fix my eyes forward in anticipation of all that is to come!

REMEMBER NOT THE FORMER THINGS, NOR CONSIDER THE THINGS OF OLD. BEHOLD, I AM DOING A NEW THING;
NOW IT SPRINGS FORTH, DO YOU NOT PERCEIVE IT? I WILL MAKE A WAY IN THE WILDERNESS AND RIVERS IN THE DESERT.
ISAIAH 43:18-19

REMEMBER NOT THE FORMER THINGS, NOR CONSIDER THE THINGS OF OLD. BEHOLD, I AM DOING A NEW THING; NOW IT SPRINGS FORTH, DO YOU NOT PERCEIVE IT? I WILL MAKE A WAY IN THE WILDERNESS AND RIVERS IN THE DESERT.
ISAIAH 43:18-19

ISAIAH 43:22-44:5

DEVO:
JADE MOORE & LEISA GAY
DAUGHTER   MOM

Have you ever been hard hearted? Have you lived in a season where your worship felt as though you were going through the motions? You are not alone. One of the beautiful things about the Bible is that we have story after story that is relevant to us and what we are going through in life. We can be encouraged by how those before us endured and saw the Lord's great love and mercy through it all. The Israelites show us time and time again that despite their sin, disbelief, and hard heartedness, God still loved them! He longs for His people to humble themselves and return to Him.

My mom and I were talking about seasons where we have been hardhearted, meaning there was indifference in our belief of who Christ is. There are times when we've been unmerciful in our approach to situations, and the bottom line is that there was no reverence for Christ and what He did for us on the cross. Similarly, the Israelites lost their reverence toward the Lord in their time in the wasteland. I love how the Message translation paraphrases this rebuke against them:

"But you didn't pay a bit of attention to me, Jacob.
You so quickly tired of me, Israel.
You wouldn't even bring sheep for offerings in worship.
You couldn't be bothered with sacrifices.
It wasn't that I asked that much from you.
I didn't expect expensive presents.
But you didn't even do the minimum—
so stingy with me, so closefisted.
Yet you haven't been stingy with your sins.
You've been plenty generous with them—and I'm fed up."
Isaiah 43:22-24 MSG

I am more of a point-blank person. Please do not beat around the bush or add a lot of fluff to a conversion when you are trying to correct or point something out! When I read this, I feel seen, but I also feel exposed. When my heart was hard, it was easier to turn away from living as a fully devoted follower of Christ. I could come to church and just do what was expected without much emotional investment or recognition of why I was even there. My heart was calloused, and therefore unable to see the spiral of complacency I was choosing to live in.

In the CSB translation, verse 22 says, "But Jacob, you have not called on me because, Israel, you have become weary of me." The word "weary" is repeated 3 times in this passage. The Lord is calling them out for their sleepy, bored, and exhausted hearts towards Him. How do we get to a place like this? We forget. Unfortunate situations or circumstances present themselves, and we forget. Thankfully, the mercy of God supersedes our forgetfulness with scripture like this to stand on.

"Consider him who endured such opposition from sinners, so that you will not grow weary and lose heart." **Hebrews 12:3**

"You have persevered and have endured hardships for my name, and have not grown weary." **Revelation 2:3**

We are to consider Him. He says we have persevered and have endured hardships for His name. The emphasis is HIM. Addressing the hard heart often involves an inward reflection and a willingness to see things in a different perspective. David says it like this:

"Search me, God, and know my heart; test me and know my anxious thoughts." **Psalm 139:23**

Hard heartedness is a barrier to growth and enlightenment; however, the power that is at work within us, the wonder-working power of Jesus Christ, can help us overcome. If you are asking yourself, "Do I have a hard heart?" I believe the Lord will reveal to you where He wants to restore and renew. It's one question, one step, closer to better understanding the deep desire God has to just be with you.

HOW THE LORD DEALS WITH A HARDENED HEART

"I, only I, am He who wipes out your transgressions for My own sake, and I will not remember your sins. Remind Me [of your merits with a thorough report], let us plead and argue our case together; state your position, that you may be proved right." Isaiah 43:25-26 (AMP)

The phrase "wipes out" is said 36 times in 32 verses. He will wipe out your sins the same way He wiped out mankind and animals in Genesis when He commissioned Noah to build a boat. An entire nation, erased. This means an entire lifetime of sin—past, present, and future—removed, because He chooses to. Our sins are plentiful, but His love is so profound that it cannot be contained or measured by ordinary standards.

To be honest, this has been difficult for me to wrap my head around. I have a hard heart—I choose to not believe or trust the Lord—and yet, He longs for my humble return, wants to forgive me, and chooses to forget my sin. Titus 3:5 says,

"He saved us, not because of righteous things we had done, but because of his mercy. He saved us through the washing of rebirth and renewal by the Holy Spirit."

He saved us because of His mercy. This means when God made the covenant with Abraham— the promised land, descendants, and a promise of hope and restoration—He was going to keep His word. When we turn to the Lord, or rather, turn back to the Lord, He wants us to partake in His goodness.

SPIRITUAL BLESSING

"But now listen, Jacob, my servant,
Israel, whom I have chosen.
This is what the Lord says—
he who made you, who formed you in the womb,
and who will help you:
Do not be afraid, Jacob, my servant,
Jeshurun, whom I have chosen.
For I will pour water on the thirsty land,
and streams on the dry ground;
I will pour out my Spirit on your offspring,
and my blessing on your descendants.
They will spring up like grass in a meadow,
like poplar trees by flowing streams.
Some will say, 'I belong to the Lord';
others will call themselves by the name of Jacob;
still others will write on their hand, 'The Lord's,'
and will take the name Israel."
Isaiah 44:1-5

I'm a bit of a plant lady. I by no means could tell you the names of plants, or how much water or light certain ones need, but I'm willing to let Google tell me as needed. Certain plants don't require a lot of water or attention, which goes well for me and our busy household. But somehow, most plants that I have acquired over the years need all the water, and all the attention. I can relate; I am much like the needy plants and forgetful Israelites. When I am doing well, the climate is right, the soil is healthy, and I'm positioned correctly to receive light, I'm good. But when I am off, whew... I am weary, dry, dark, and close to being a dead plant in a pot.

In our time today, we have gone through the calling out of the Israelites, and ourselves, to then allow the incomprehensible love of our Lord and His desire to be with us knock off the hardened places of our hearts. Now, we get to receive the blessing promised to not just simply give us His spirit, but to pour it out!

The pouring out is not subtle, but evident. It implies that God's presence through the Spirit should be noticeable in the lives of those who receive it, displaying in actions, thoughts, and spiritual growth. Whether someone is experiencing only a small measure of the Spirit, feels completely dry, or is already familiar with its effects, the message is clear: God's desire is to continue pouring out His Spirit. This is an invitation to seek a deeper relationship with God and to expect more of His presence.

Sister, you were made and formed. You will be helped, and you are chosen. Do not be afraid! If you are thirsty and dry, He wants to pour out His spirit on you. He wants to bless your children and their children; because of that, the evidence of God's great love and mercy for you and your family will quicken you to remember the Lord. When you recognize the hardened heart returning, this powerful message about the abundance and continual outpouring of the Holy Spirit will emphasize the limitless nature of God's blessings. Trust in His timing and generosity. Don't passively wait, but actively participate in His transformative plan.

✹ REFLECTION:

1. Are you in a season where your heart is hard? If so, share with someone who can partner with you and pray for freedom.
2. Is there any area where you do not believe your sins have been wiped out? Why? (If yes, write them down and pray a prayer of repentance. The Lord wants to set you free!)
3. Have you put limitations or conditions on receiving the pouring out of His Spirit?
4. Where are you seeing the evidence of the Lord "pouring out" His spirit in your life? Sharing the testimony of God's goodness in your life is encouragement to the body of Christ. Give God glory for what He has done and will continue to do!

✹ PRAYER:

Lord, I repent for forgetting. You never change, but I do, and I need You! I invite You to sweep over my soul and show me where I am hard hearted. My heart is lost and weary without You! Thank You, Lord, for Your great mercy—only You will be able to block out my sins, and I am undeserving. I recognize Your love and desire to lean into Your plan and purpose for my life. I thank You for what You did on the cross so that I can be healed and whole. I honor Your sacrifices, not just for me, but for the whole world. I will love You with my whole heart and want to live for You for all of eternity. Amen.

**REMEMBER NOT THE FORMER THINGS, NOR CONSIDER THE THINGS OF OLD. BEHOLD, I AM DOING A NEW THING;
NOW IT SPRINGS FORTH, DO YOU NOT PERCEIVE IT? I WILL MAKE A WAY IN THE WILDERNESS AND RIVERS IN THE DESERT.
ISAIAH 43:18-19**

REMEMBER NOT THE FORMER THINGS, NOR CONSIDER THE THINGS OF OLD. BEHOLD, I AM DOING A NEW THING; NOW IT SPRINGS FORTH, DO YOU NOT PERCEIVE IT? I WILL MAKE A WAY IN THE WILDERNESS AND RIVERS IN THE DESERT.
ISAIAH 43:18-19

ISAIAH
44:6-8

DEVO:
HEATHER HOYT, REBECCA SHATSWELL, & JULIE HOYT
DAUGHTERS   MOM

"This is what the Lord says—Israel's King and Redeemer, the Lord Almighty: I am the first and I am the last; apart from me there is no God. Who then is like me? Let him proclaim it. Let him declare and lay out before me what has happened since I established my ancient people, and what is yet to come—yes, let them foretell what will come. Do not tremble, do not be afraid. Did I not proclaim this and foretell it long ago? You are my witnesses. Is there any God besides me? No, there is no other Rock; I know not one."

Isaiah 44:6-8

In these verses, God is closing out an important message to His people. Although they have experienced much hardship because of their sin and disregard for Him, now He is doing something **NEW**. He is moving to redeem them, lead them, and pour out His Spirit upon them that they might be refreshed and bring Him glory once again.

THREE TIMES, HE SAYS "DO NOT FEAR:"
- **Do not fear;** I have redeemed you from your past (Isa 43:1)
- **Do not fear;** I am with you in the hard or unknown (Isa 43:5)
- **Do not fear;** I will pour out My Spirit to give you fresh life (Isa 44:2-3)

He puts His exclamation point in the last 3 verses (Isa 44:6-8) by declaring that He alone is God and there is no other like Him! He says, "I am the first and the last," meaning He is before and after everything. He exists outside of time itself! He is the prequel and the sequel. This means everything— you, and I, and all creation—find ourselves in the middle of HIS story.

A few years ago, my sister was tasked with training her new boss at work. I chuckled at the awkwardness of the scenario. Sensing her mixed emotions, I listened as she processed her thoughts. While some might jump at the opportunity to influence their leader, she felt equal parts confusion and fear mixed with the discomfort of knowing more than her superior in this area. And let's be honest, it would be really hard to navigate "bossing" your boss. Outwardly, I was both supportive and thankful it wasn't my responsibility, but inwardly I began to wrestle, wondering how often I had spoken to God as though my days outnumbered His...as if my experience needed to be revealed to Him... as if I could instruct Him.

Don't we want a God who existed before our days began and who will infinitely outlast our final breaths on earth? Isn't there comfort in being led, not by some incoming untrained boss we're responsible to instruct, but by the Creator who has neither beginning nor end, who laid the foundations of the earth and holds the entirety of our timelines in His hands? The answer—yes! Everyone wants a God like this!

"I am the first and the last," God declares of Himself through Isaiah. Now, fast forward to the book of Revelation. We see that our glorious King Jesus, years after He ascended to heaven, comes to the apostle John and introduces (actually re-introduces) Himself with these same words: "Do not be afraid. I am the First and the Last. I am the Living One; I was dead, and now look, I am alive for ever and ever" (Rev 1:17-18). Jesus of the New Testament refers to Himself by the very same name God spoke to Isaiah over 800 years prior.

This means that Jesus Himself was speaking to Isaiah in the Old Testament, before He was born on Earth, declaring that He is the beginning and the end and He alone is God. What?!? Jesus made a cameo appearance in the Old Testament—a sneak peak of His glory to come. He really is the First and the Last! And then in Isaiah 44:8, He invites us to personally wrestle with this truth: "Is there any God besides Me?"

The obvious answer is no. No other leader or prophet or false deity comes close to the One who is BEFORE all and AFTER all, the One who entered the very world He created to die in our place...the one who took off His crown and chose the cross.

And while Jesus has no parallel or rival, the real question is, do we have anyone or thing that competes with or rivals Him in our lives? Do we have something or someone beside or even in front of Him? Is He our FIRST and our LAST? Let's stop and ask the Holy Spirit to search us.

✸ REFLECTION:

1. Who or what do I put before Jesus?
2. What do I turn to first and last in my day?
3. What is God leading me to do in obedience to Him?
4. Who can I share this with so that I will truly walk this out?

✸ PRAYER:

Lord Jesus, You are such an awesome God! There is no other! I marvel at the works of Your hands. Before creation, You were there. There is none like You!

Forgive me for when I have chosen other things before You. I repent of giving other things first place or the main focus of my life. Help me to love You with all my heart, mind, and strength, and then to love people from the overflow of Your love! Thank You for loving me before I even called Your name!

How comforting it is to know You are ever present and constant. You hold every answer to my needs! I will not tremble or be afraid because I trust in You. You are God and there is no other—thank You, Lord!

REMEMBER NOT THE FORMER THINGS, NOR CONSIDER THE THINGS OF OLD. BEHOLD, I AM DOING A NEW THING:
NOW IT SPRINGS FORTH. DO YOU NOT PERCEIVE IT? I WILL MAKE A WAY IN THE WILDERNESS AND RIVERS IN THE DESERT.
ISAIAH 43:18-19

REMEMBER NOT THE FORMER THINGS, NOR CONSIDER THE THINGS OF OLD. BEHOLD, I AM DOING A NEW THING;
NOW IT SPRINGS FORTH, DO YOU NOT PERCEIVE IT? I WILL MAKE A WAY IN THE WILDERNESS AND RIVERS IN THE DESERT.
ISAIAH 43:18-19

BIBLE STUDY RESOURCES

VIDEO DEVOTIONALS
Scan this QR code to go deeper each week with a short video devotional.

As you further study God's word, we wanted to provide you with online Bible study tools that will help deepen your understanding of scripture. Some of our favorites are:

BIBLE GATEWAY
BIBLE HUB
BIBLE PROJECT
BIBLE STUDY TOOLS
BLUE LETTER BIBLE
SHE READS TRUTH
THE BIBLE RECAP

We also have extended study options available through our Learning & Development program at New Life Church!

The School of Ministry at New Life Church is a two-year program designed to equip and empower those who are called to lead their homes, communities, cities, churches, and the world toward becoming fully devoted followers of Christ.

NLC College combines the strong tradition, Christian development, and liberal arts education of Southeastern University with the life-giving ministry of New Life Church to offer a truly unique educational experience. Students earn a fully accredited associate, bachelor's or master's degree.

For more information about these programs, visit newlifechurch.tv.

FOLLOW US ON INSTAGRAM

 @womanconference
@newlifechurchtv

Made in the USA
Columbia, SC
25 September 2024

43032467R00027